Rudolf G. Binding · Equestrian Hymn for my Beloved

Documenta Hippologica

Darstellungen und Quellen zur Geschichte des Pferdes

Founded by
Oberst H. Handler, H. J. Köhler,
E. v. Neindorff, Dr. B. Schirg,
Oberst W. Seunig, Dr. W. Uppenborn,
Dr. G. Wenzler

Edited by
Brigadier K. Albrecht, Spanische Hofreitschule,
General P. Durand, Cadre Noir,
Prof. Dr. E.-H. Lochmann,
Dr. N. Záliš, T. Frei

Olms Presse
Hildesheim · Zürich · New York
2006

Rudolf G. Binding

Equestrian Hymn
for my Beloved

Translated by
Regina Ganstine

With a preface by
Erik Herbermann

and photos
by Rik Van Lent, Jr.

Ǫ

Olms Presse
Hildesheim · Zürich · New York
2006

Die Deutsche Bibliothek lists this publication
in the Deutsche Nationalbibliographie,
detailed bibliographic data are available in the
Internet at http://dnb.ddb.de.

∞ ISO 9706
Printed in Germany
Cover Design: Paul König, Hildesheim, Germany
© Georg Olms Verlag AG, Hildesheim 2006
All rights reserved
ISBN 3-487-08458-9
ISSN 0175-9108

This translation is dedicated to Regina Ganstine

She will always be in our hearts

Regina Petra Ganstine was born of Oskar and Louise
Charlotte Krapat in Mannheim, Germany on November 27, 1957.
Affected deeply by the death of her father at age 10, she found
solace in her passion for horses. As a woman, Regina worked
tirelessly as a Certified Public Translator to create the means
by which she would realize her dream of owning, riding,
and breeding the most beautiful animal in the world, the horse.
Her credits as a Translator are many, the highlight being her
September 13, 2004 translation for German Chancellor Gerhard Schroeder
during a press conference including the leaders of Germany, Spain, and France.
Her talent for language met her devotion to horses in her translation
of "Equestrian Hymn for My Beloved," a self-described labor of love.
She died on November 10, 2004 shortly after completing the translation,
a work which best conveys her spirit and how it was affected
in the presence of the horse.

Carey T. Ramirez, son of Regina Ganstine

Regina Ganstine

FOREWORD

This is the most extraordinary and worthwhile little book. It was created, unmistakably, by one who felt to the core of his being the need for noble purpose in human endeavor. With masterful brevity, Rudolf G. Binding's words soar into the realm of timelessness as they deftly penetrate and unravel to the most profound elements of the horse's nature.

Rudolf G. Binding (1867 - 1938) was born in Basel, Switzerland. Even before he became known as a respected poet and author in Germany literary circles, he was acknowledged as a man of refined stature and demeanour when he held the position of Riding Master in the "Grimmaer Koenigin-Husaren" during the First World War. As decommissioned officer after the war he was temporarily Mayor of Buchschlag-Spredlingen near Darmstadt, after which he lived near Lake Starnberg. Besides this book and other equestrian work, Das Heiligtum der Pferde (The Sanctum of Horses), Binding wrote largely traditionalistic material, with emphasis on sacrifice and heroism, and legends of his time. He was best known for his novels: Opfergang 1912 (Sacrificial Path); Unsterblichkeit 1921 (Immortality); Erlebtes Leben 1928 (A Life Lived); and Moselfahrt aus Liebeskummer 1932 (Sailing the Mosel

Photo by H. Reinhard

in Love's Distress). The brief pages of Equestrian Hymn for my Beloved were likely never meant to be published, but were indeed an equestrian guideline for the author's loved one. It is filled with wisdom, sensitivity and passion for all that is beautiful and worthy in horsemanship. It is inspiring, illuminating, and instructive – equestrian holy writ, with which to be familiar and to honor, if a deep and harmonious relationship with the horse is to be cultivated, and if horsemanship is to transcend beyond the mediocrity of technical craft.

The translation from the original German text by Regina Ganstine (1957 - 2004) is, simply put, exquisite. She was herself a devoted rider and advocate of classical horsemanship. And because of her comfort with both languages, the English text retains the depth, transparency and richness of the original German. Translating this work had special significance for Regina; it was a true labor of love for her – one she unfortunately never got to see published.

Irrespective of the equestrian discipline one might choose to follow, I wholeheartedly recommend this succinct volume to all riders who wish to expand and refine their understanding of the creature they so love.

Erik Herbermann, Karlsruhe 2005

Photo by Rik Van Lent, Jr.

C ome! On your horse! Come, embrace the sunshine and the air. Leave the dusty arena with its corners and confinement to those who think small. Come to freedom, the orbit of eternity, where untouched grass is covered with dew, where shadows of foliage dance across your path, where light caresses you, where the wind toys with you, where there are no limits, where your heart opens wide as you ride into its boundless domain.

Because, this my beloved, is my prophecy: Your horse's back will put the world at your feet. I want to make it your throne from which you shall carry a scepter of power, of joy, and of freedom, as you never dreamed possible.

O nly outside will your horse carry you as it was meant to be – if you love. Only outside under the open skies will he be royal, will he be all beast. Only outside will he be truly alive. Only if he obeys you outside, will he be completely at your will. Only outside will he feel his full power, will you too feel his total power.

Perpetually tracking through corners, gaits imprisoned in ever diminishing circles, nailed ramps and guards, a roof to conceal the sky – is this fit for lovers?

Haute École – oh well, that may be. But what about the highest of teachings? Do you really wish to foreclose them? My beloved, only the heavens are great enough to be your firmament when you ride.

N ow that your horse is carrying you, do not listen so much to me as you listen to your horse. Your horse will be your ultimate teacher. He is your schoolmaster who will discipline and reward: he will close his heart to you if you follow doctrines other than his own. Learn from your horse.

Riding becomes unadulterated joy only after you have traveled a path of many arduous lessons in patience, tactfulness, and energy, with your horse as lecturer.

Don't spend your time studying rules of riding and don't emulate professional riders.

They know of nothing but their craft, but riding is not a craftsman's trade, it is an art.

Equestrian regulations of the ordinary kind are much like piano tutors; they teach riding as a learned skill that can be taught: like sewing and mending socks.

Listen to your horse closely, as you would listen to a valuable instrument, like Elly Ney listens to her grand piano, Busch to his violin, Barjansky to his cello. Wondrous wisdom will be yours far exceeding the realm of riding schools, or equerries.

Photo by Rik Van Lent, Jr.

All of the virtues proclaimed by the riding masters cannot serve as a substitute for the sweet, gentle chattering of your horse when, on a beautiful summer morning, he takes his first steps into freedom under you, as he searches for your hand with feeling lips, seeking contact with the bit as he stretches into the reins, as he softly inquires and questioningly probes, as he then plays with the finely tuned steel bar in his mouth, pushing it away ever so little in deliberation, and as he leans against it ever so slightly as if to put it to the test, to then accept it with a long neck, with his poll elevated, his head unconfined, and with gentle play of his tongue, as if he was accepting a gift bestowed upon him on which he may be proud. Your horse is happy then.

Regina Ganstine

Be the enemy of the spirit of heavyheartedness. This will allow your horse to carry you in lightness. When your heart is light, so is your hand. When your heart is light it will drive you forward. Those who are melancholy in spirit and deprived of hope or courage are propelled by nothing. But, forward movement is everything.

When your horse resists, he does so out of the spirit of stagnation, of regression. When you are able to drive the resistant horse forward do not relent in this half the battle is won. This is because he must expend a part of his power in the forward movement you are asking of him, and only the other part remains for his resistance. Bucking and kicking, rearing and tossing himself to the ground are easily overcome in forward movement, but are insurmountable at a standstill.

Nobody else will teach you as thoroughly as the resistant horse that moving forward is everything.

Be a friend of the spirit of weightlessness. Those who move in suspension will always be in balance. Stay with your horse like a bird on the back of the air which carries it. This is the bird's secret, make it your own. Those who soar don't fall.

But, even if you do fall, remain with your horse. Remain with him like the bird on the air which drops out from under him. In doing so, you will find yourself received more gently by the earth, wherever you meet it.

But your eyes must be open and your senses must not desert you.

Photo by H. Reinhard

R iding is willpower for that which is afar, for infinity. If your soul, united with the power of your horse, perceives anything other than infinity and joyfulness as it is carried into the morning and sunshine, it does not recognize the full splendor of this secret.

But it is your horse's ears which are at play at the periphery of this infinity.

Photo by Rik Van Lent, Jr.

B e on guard: your horse reads you and your most secret thoughts. If you are not intent on reigning over him, he will not obey you; if it is not your will to be stronger, the extraordinary power of the beast will defy you. Your call, your click of the tongue, your spurs, your whip shall not belie you; you wanted this or that, but you only wanted it halfway.

Your horse will punish you for lying.

If you do not trust him he will not trust you;

if you waver, he will go his own way.

If you panic, he will panic; but he will be filled with courage and good spirit if you are courageous and in good spirit.

If you are unsteady, he will be unsteady. If your will is not set on perpetual forward motion, he will slow down and eventually stand still.

If you are without vigor, he will be without impulsion; if you wish to fly, he will fly, his feet will hardly seem to touch the ground.

A suspended formation of live steel seems to be carrying you. But if you allow yourself to be fought to the ground in spirit and in willpower, a listless worm will be crawling under you in the dust.

Your horse knows everthing about you: he knows whether you slept well the night before, whether you are absentminded or concentrated, whether you are happy or sad, whether you are confident or full of doubts, whether your mind is set on riding, or on breakfast.

Those who despise the earth, those who are not in love with the horizon, those who are petty and small, those who are marked by dishonesty, those who are not of clear spirit, those who are doubtful, those who are negative, will ride poorly. Those who are driven straightforward, those who seek life, those who are leaders and in command of themselves most of the time, those who are calm and collected within themselves, those who have confidence in themselves while being of clear spirit, may ride well. Riding is an endless affirmation, and this is especially true when your horse seems to deny your will.

You must become one with your horse. When he carries you on his back you cannot allow yourself to be separated from him, neither in visible fashion nor in your own thought. He will not belong to you unless you belong to him.

Your relationship with your horse is not a marriage by which two parties can be united whether they belong together or not, where one walks beside the other without knowing any more about him than the everyday mundane.

Reflect on this: your friend's strength is greater than yours, and yet you are his mistress. Reflect on how this came about for your horse's mistress you shall be.

You are being carried by the most lovable, most sensitive animal ever created. Know this. Never disregard this and while you never disregard this, draw upon it to your best advantage. You cannot be effective with pressure and force of your leg or knee (the action of which is far less than other forces, even with your seat spread over the back of your horse). The side-saddle seat on one flank will especially deprive you of this influence. However, for your full seat, you have traded the advantages of a long rein and, by nature, you have a lighter and more sensitive hand.

So take effect through delicacy, you who are capable of all feeling. No animal will be more grateful and no animal will appreciate this more than your horse.

I f you did not have the hands of a lady, I would wish for you the hands of a child. I have watched the most famous and best jockey of a decade – the life of a celebrated jockey in his glamour hardly ever lasts longer than that – I have watched him with his childlike hands on the race track between the spectators and the bleachers where gigantic thoroughbreds were being saddled, where he paraded around the winner's circle with his whip and then – all of 11 years old at the time – his trainer put him on top of these mighty animals like a tiny living burdock. He would guide them securely by that proverbial thread of silk. And, with all of the exuberance that only 2-year-olds can muster up as they enter the race track for the first time, none of them ever ran away with him, or became unmanageable. The hands of the child pleased them.

Will you not surpass the hands of the child in their tenderness?

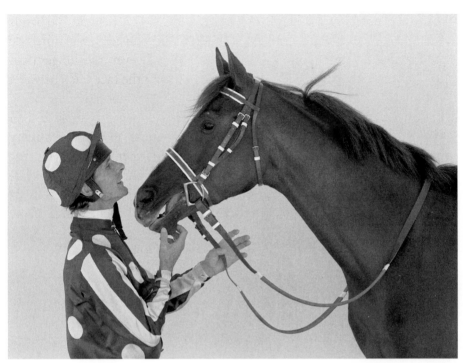

Photo by Rik Van Lent, Jr.

What wonderful gentle play and interaction of the human hand and the horse's lips. Have you ever given this any thought? It is as if the beast was smitten with your light and soulful resistance, just as the resistance of your soul might delight your lover. This is life. If you ride as it was meant to be, your horse will unceasingly seek this charming play with you in forward impulsion. The more your hand reaches ahead of him, the more persistently and eagerly the animal will seek it – for the sake of playing with you.

Gently nudge your horse forward into this play as he moves. His neck will lengthen then. To follow the hand he loves, his stride will lengthen, swing, while, at the same time, becoming more rhythmic and larger. His whole body will strive to reach the point of contact where the game is played, where he can feel it: his hindlegs step under his rising back with greater zealousness. His ears point forward. His poll elevates. His neck is raised freely from his shoulder.

The entire vertebral column from his tail to his poll is arched into an elastic, resilient bridge, stretched into freedom until it comes to rest on the bar of the bit at its incomparable point of support which always reaches ahead of him, and which is as consistent and light as a dancer as she floats across the floor in the arms of her partner.

However, it is not play, but crude violation with powerful levers driving those who resist the horse's mouth as he seeks that sensitive hand; he will seek to evade this, even if he moves hesitantly forward. Then, his neck will shorten instead of becoming longer, his ears will be laid back, his nose will drop against his chest, his poll will lower and his gaits will shorten. The riding instructor with dilettante concepts will tell you that he is pushing himself off the bit. But what is really happening is that the hand pushes the horse away, repulses it.

Photo by Rik Van Lent, Jr.

M y beloved, have you in your mind ever reflected upon the wonderful instrument which is resting in the mouth of your horse in the form of a steel mouthpiece with its two shanks while, at the same time, surrounding his lower jaw with a curb chain for play? It is probably rare that anyone would still be mindful of the genius behind this tool, just as people no longer are aware of what a wheel represents, what a pair of pliers or a cylinder is. The curb bit is a trigger for all of the levers in the horse's body. From the right perspective, it controls all of his joints in their entirety, but it has been deprived of its original inherent magic. Only you might resurrect that magic once again.

Perhaps a noble Arab Sheik dreamed it up in his vision and association with the utmost impulsion of a wellbred horse. Perhaps, he ordered it to be made by a skillful blacksmith of his tribe, who had a sense for what was of the essence here.

Photo by Rik Van Lent, Jr.

Only the Arab has treated this instrument in the spirit in which it was invented from time immemorial; but the armored fist of the medieval knight, the running attack against his opponent in the tournaments on coarse ironclad horses stripped this invention of the refined gracefulness behind its original intent, to act as the horse's support and aid him in free movement which was almost detached from the ground. So, what is happening here? When he would step into the opening of his tent, that Arab would see his young noble horse grazing at liberty on the desert grasses, and hurrying towards him when he called. His movements would be afloat with strength, inquisitiveness, and yearning for the hand which might perhaps present him with a treat. My horse does not move like this under the weight of my body, he said to himself. How can I alleviate that weight, what can I give to my horse, so that he will not feel my weight any more? So that he will move with this kind of weightlessness under me? And he resorted to thinking up a support for him which would consistently remain in front of him in this elevated carriage, which would make it easier for his horse to carry his own weight in his movement even with the load of his rider's weight on his back.

That is when he consulted with his blacksmith.

Because it was invented for energetic movement, the bit is only effective in energetic motion. After all, what sense would it make to add support to a horse that is resting on his legs? Compared to the flying Arab Sheik, don't many of today's riders, like the ungainly memorial statues of a few rulers astride on their horses, appear quite pitiful when they find pleasure in standing at a halt while thoughtlessly and insensitively allowing the curb to act upon their horses' jaw? This works indeed; but because there is no energy to be absorbed, no movement which it supports, it turns into an absurdity. Would people not laugh if a dancer's partner attempted to support her by pressing against her with his finger while she was standing next to him on the floor? This is how the curb presses against the horse at the halt. Because he will not fall over so easily, his head alone will evade the lever action by approaching his chest. His nose is pulled in, but this occurs without the sense this process might make while he is moving.

Because there is no action to step under them, the poll and neck are no longer elastic, the arched tensile stretch which, in motion, is shared with all of the vertebrae of the spinal cord, flexes and rolls itself up, and the most ingenious invention of the horseman's spirit is robbed of its effectiveness. Never has an instrument in human hands been so misconceived as this revelation of the orient in the hands of occidental riders.

Leave it to the descendants of the mounted knights, the Christians and the Jews, to abuse and break the necks of their horse through forceful lever action. But you, my beloved, you must remember the Sheik and his vision.

Photo by C. Toischel

You shall only ride the most finely bred horses. Select your horse as you would select your lover for you shall love your horse. And, as you would only select your lover among the noblest and finest, you shall choose your horse in the same way.

You shall have an inner vision of your horse, even before you make him your own.

Photo by Rik Van Lent, Jr.

The creatures of the earth are looking at you in their great diversity. Some of them will share their lives with you. But the horse who carries you may be the most magnificent of all to you.

His eye will be an ocean of tranquility in which a bloodstream of nobility and strength has been collected for centuries. He will look around himself with calmness and attentiveness, and he will also register your presence as you stop to look at him from a distance. His ears are engaged in reflective play, they are alert and often quietly pointed forward; his nostrils are delicate and tender; his lips are thin, his tongue invisible; at this moment, neither saliva nor froth is wetting his mouth.

His head is painstakingly chiseled, his nose straight and narrow. His neck is carried in a long line, freely, and with ease, and emerges from a shoulder which is upright and close to his body, while it is not pressed apart by his powerful rump. His chest is not excessively broad but deep, and no fat or heavy tissue is deposited on his shoulder. His withers are narrow (but not excessively pointed), strong, and wellshaped, and, like a band, it extends into his elastic wellmuscled back. Rest your gaze on this spot for some time.

This spot, closely behind the withers, near his shoulder, will carry you. This part of him must literally invite you to take a seat. It is short, but within it, a deep and inexplorable chest cavity encloses the heart and lungs.

But the line of his back does not seem to want to end. His pelvis is long and reaches well under him. He is carrying his tail freely and calmly.

Longstretched, straight hindlegs strive towards the earth from his stifle, which you regard from the front. All of his joints are as if they had been embossed, strong, and clearly delineated. A delicate and well defined network of blood vessels is markedly discernible under his fine skin. You can almost scan the tendons of his front legs and hocks with your naked eye, down to the solid and elastic pasterns over his round feet at rest.

Equipped in this fashion, your horse, in consideration of his noble birth of ancient aristocracy, steps outside over the threshold of his stall with almost regal dignity. His step is secure and light. The eternal fire of the desert flows within his veins. His blood is pure, overflowing with tried and tested, carefully selected ancestors. His manners are perfect. He was already a riding horse while still in his dam's womb.

Photo by W. Georg Olms

D o you love to dance?
Your horse is a dancer in your hands, a dancer into infinity. From the impulsion you impart on him, lightness will follow, weightlessness will follow. You feel him unite all of his power under your saddle. You leave the land behind you. The world flows by. Your dancer is carrying you away.

M ay the vision of your horse's image follow you by day and by night, while you are awake and while you are asleep, as if it were the image of your lover which haunts you. His form must be indestructible, lasting, and eternal like a painting by Tiziano Vencellio, like a sculpted statue by Praxiteles. If, overnight, he escapes your innermost being, or even if he merely fades, if his shape becomes distorted, he is not the horse that I mean.

Optically conspicuous horses are unbecoming to a lady. Ride horses who become you. You might select your gown to be ornate and glamorous for certain occasions, but you will never select it to be gaudy. As your riding dress shall be uniform in color, so shall your horse be of one color. Leave colorful horses, chestnuts with blazes and lots of white on their legs to the coquettes and cocottes.

You shall ride horses of a deep brown color, blackbrown, red, or gold.

You shall only ride unspoiled horses, and you shall guard their innocence. This is what I interpret as an inner unmarked purity, which consists in that, in spite of his obedience, and in spite of his perhaps highest levels of training, none of his natural freshness, trust, and love of forward movement has been lost.

This, my beloved, is because your own soul has its innate innocence and may you preserve it – forever.

Do you believe that it is life which breaks a man's spirit? Just look at what humans make out of their horses. It is man who breaks life. And that is how man also breaks the life of the horse's spirit.

The wretched effect of commonly practiced dressage: his dressage training is complete, but his life is gone. Punishment and gagging devices, horses being pulled together between perpetually blocking reins and perpetually driving legs and spurs, cursed auxiliary reins, endless standing in place, horses being driven up to merciless columns (pillars), the monstrous joylessness of our schoolmasters' trade has broken him. You are merely sitting on a wellconditioned machine any more.

Photo by N. Reinhard

No effort of yours will be great enough to succeed in bringing joy to your horse again. Your courting is in vain. He will not dance under you, smile under you, he will no longer play with you. Nothing will search for you. Your horse is obedient out of habituation, because he no longer knows of anything else.

Just watch highly bred foals and yearlings as they run at liberty in the fields. It may be true that, as they run with the herd, they are without care and may even slouch about. But when self-confidence gets a hold of them, when they show off and put on, they float around with elevated strides. They have fire under their feet. They fly. Their whole body is carried in suspension, an interaction of triggers in all joints at the same time. They support themselves lightly on an invisible bridle with their arched, elevated necks. The whole animal seems to be stepping under the arch of his neck. An invisible rider's hand follows it in gaits never taught, into natural Haute École. This shall be your aspiration – and you will know what an innocent horse is, what innocent horses are capable of.

Photo by Doris Melzer

As you ride out of the stableyard, do not take up the reins before you have not given your horse the gift of freedom to look around in the morning into which he is carrying you. Allow him this freedom that you yourself enjoy. If he stretches out his neck as long as he wants, points his ears, his eyes gazing calmly at his surroundings at large, as he flares his nostrils, how often will a smile in his soul be reaching out for the morning air. Do not withhold that from him.

Think that you yourself are sitting more erect, that you open your chest, and that you are breathing deeply before the richness of the day.

Minds racing in sleepless nights, stomach ills, indigestion after gluttony, bloating, wishes denied, unsatisfied cravings, these are the things that man will transfer to his horse's back. But you, my beloved, shall place warm thoughts of the morning, the taste of kisses on your mouth, the afterglow of pleasure, and a slender body on your horse's back.

When you are on your horse, be charming and your horse will be graceful.

Your horse is not that sharp of mind and not all that obedient; he will hardly do anything for his rider because he understands him or the so-called aids of the stable master's teaching habits, or because he will listen to them. However, the horse is enormously receptive to suggestiveness; he will be led by your will first and last. But you must have that will.

He is fickle; so you must be free of fickleness. He has little devotion, so you must be devoted. He does not care who feeds him, who whips him, so you must prove to him that this does matter, that your will is foremost. He will tend to try to make a stand here and there when this is convenient to him, but not with his physical strength – because he would always win against yours – but instead, he will often do so with childlike defiance, so you must reign over him with the sovereignty of your innermost being.

Photo by Rik Van Lent, Jr.

It is a strange misconception of those who believe that they are riding when they are never quite able to conquer their fear, when they are happy to be carried about. Will the horse not be stronger than I, they think to themselves, because they will always feel that they are separated from him. How do I look, they ask themselves with concern, and would give a lot to be able to look into a mirror, or to view their reflection in a shop window.

Miserable, Madam, it does not matter how correctly you try to sit, we answer, as we pass on our horses.

In her acquaintance with horses, she is more motivated by vanity than by her love of the horse.

Photo by Rik Van Lent, Jr.

Only choose well-mannered men as your companions. By this, I mean men who are well-mannered with their horses. If they are true horsemen inside and out, they will also not behave poorly towards you. But if you are accompanied by people whose manners belie those of a horseman, who are not feeling as a horseman would be, then, you will grow tired of horses and riding.

Do not trust men who walk across the street wearing spurs. It is true that the spur strap is designed for strapping them on, but also to take them off. They are designed for the latter in particular. This is because, while it is correct to use the spur at the right moment when riding a horse, it is not appropriate to draw the attention of pedestrians to oneself when crossing the street. Those who conceitedly display the spurs on their boots will surely not know how to use them. If people will not mock them, their horses will certainly laugh at them.

Carry your spurs in your hand as you walk to the stable, and do not strap them on until the time has come to mount your horse; and if you only wear them for the sake of appearance, do not strap them on at all.

Where your companion is concerned, however, may he attract attention through nothing but solid riding skills.

B e attentive to all of the secrets your horse tells you as he is carrying you. This is because your horse does have his secrets and delights in sharing them with you: trivial naughtiness, passionate tendencies, likes and dislikes, minor indiscretions, confidential truths, and perversions.

But if his rider is blind and deaf, insensitive to the emotional stirring of this living being under him, he will soon find him indifferent and stubborn, and he will say that his horse does not understand him, when in fact it is he who does not understand his horse.

If your horse is not moving well, seek within yourself. Almost invariably, you will be the reason. Notwithstanding, I have seen riders dismount and fearfully inspect their horse's belly – as if it had been a fly which kept him from jumping the ditch in front of which he just stopped while stomping his hindlegs in objection.

Despise those who state: I do not know what was the matter with the stubborn pig today, that he moved so poorly, that he did not want to cross the creek, that he turned around by the wind mill. Ask yourself whether your hand was light, your confidence unfazed. Was it not you who refused to jump over the water? Were you not fearful that your horse might shy away from the rattling paddles of the wind mill?

Your horse is your mirror. He will never flatter you in vain. He will reflect your character. He will also reflect your strengths and weaknesses. Never become angry with your horse for you might as well be annoyed with your mirror.

You should never ride short of your ability. Most people ride below their skill level. All of their moods, their grudges, business gone awry, and their anger with themselves, they take out on their horses — even if they are frequently unaware that this is what they are doing. They ride worse on uneven paths than on smooth footing although only the horse will feel the hardness of the rocks. In storms and in rain, they will hang to one side like slouches, lopsided and sloppily; they will ride more poorly alone than in the company of others who may be observing them.

On horseback, the weather is always better than on foot.

Photo by Rik Van Lent, Jr.

D o not keep your horse in a dark stall for 22 hours of a 24-hour day, leaving him to stare at the painted walls to then chase him about outside for two hours only to lock him up again. If this were to be done to you, this would also make you dull and gloomy, excitable and unruly. Instead, after your ride in the morning, take your horse out of his stall once more in the evening – without his saddle or bridle. Take an evening walk with him to the edge of the meadow, or between the patches of grass along the road; allow him to feast on a few handfuls of fresh clover, green grass, talk with him a little, do not object as he rubs his head against your hand – and lead him home again.

On some evenings, a little child may take him for a walk in your place, but you shall never esteem too lightly the service you provide your horse.

B e demanding of your horse. Undemanding riders gloss over their inability. Do not only demand that he carries you. Demand that he carries you securely, without any visible aids on your part. Demand of him his utmost, his best. The highest degree of good manners, attentiveness, power: demand it! Under an undemanding rider, the horse will lack good manners, he will be inattentive and slow to respond.

Always ask for a level of fine decorum, attentiveness, and strength, but only demand his greatest ability for short periods of time: one quarter hour, minutes, yes, even moments.

After a good canter in which you stretch your horse, after an energetic trot in which your horse's stride flows forward weightlessly like flashes of lightning, after a jump at maximum stretch across a creek, or in extreme collection over a rail as tall as a man, behold how your horse is proud of his work when his job has demanded his utmost power, impulsion, and agility.

Behold how he cherishes the feeling of empowerment and agility that you have given him, and have allowed him to have.

However, most people successfully prevent their horses from giving and showing their best, and everything remains stuck in a fearful short rein while the horse's neck is pulled together.

Reins do not exist to be pulled, instead, they exist for reining. All of the forward urge, all forward impulsion is destroyed when this fact is forgotten. You are violating the most sacred principles when you pull on the reins. Even an excessive forward urge of your horse should not be subjected to more rein pressure than what would be required to steer a bird. But, again and again, you will see people on horseback who seem to be measuring the strength of their arm muscles against that of the horse's shoulder and neck.

Poor manners will spoil even the best of horses. The rider's demeanor is reflected in his horse's carriage, gaits, and behavior. Just as your horse will read you, he will also reveal you.

Inconsistency, inattentiveness, affectation, petty hurriedness, idleness, moodiness, suspiciousness, maliciousness – how invariably will they be reflected back at you by your horse! Often enough, the behavior of a horse will conclusively evince his rider's personality – even if the latter is sitting at home while his horse enjoys walks on his own.

You must conquer your horse anew every day: through your love and cleverness, thoughtfulness and sovereignty, through judiciousness and courage, discipline and praise, where they are due.

Flattery will get you nowhere. The beast knows that you are not being honest, even before you yourself know it. And, embarrassed, you confess to yourself that you have employed lowly means to reach your goal. Persuasion is indeed helpful, but you shall not want to persuade your horse unless you have spurs and a whip to back up your request, along with the most indomitable willpower.

Those who ride to be transported from place to place, those who ride to engage in physical activity, those who ride for the sake of sport, and they might as well hone any other sport, do not know of the power of the horse's gaits, know nothing of their magic, know nothing of their secret.

The same body generates the walk, the trot, the canter, the racing gallop of the horse – each different in their sequence and character, in their rhythm and innate melody; how can machines measure up to this when they only know the pitch of monotone speed?

Leave it to other people to ride from here to there and back, to ride in the park to promote their digestion, tossed about, thrown up in their saddles as well as their abilities allow, mechanical shakeup of human and animal limbs. But you, my beloved, listen closely. Experience his movement. A living being is stirring under you.

Photo by Rik Van Lent, Jr.

There is his walk: the movement of serenity. He covers a lot of ground, calmly, and yet rapidly. A human being afoot following you would quickly come out of breath, would begin to jog even if he only intended to remain by your side for 15 minutes. But your horse is unhurried. He turns his head a little, even his neck; his long reins permit him to do so. He has time.

The hoofbeat on the pavement is a flowing, pronounced, and clearly cadenced fourbeat rhythm. He steps forward and under himself twice, alternating distinctly. The rhythm envelops you. This is no time for daydreaming. His pace is melodic like ringing bells which accompany you on your way.

But only if you are collected within your soul, serene, and without hidden agendas, if you are taken in by this huge and tranquil movement, if you seek to be fast by covering ground, and not by rushing, will his walk be the walk that becomes you.

B ut, soon, quiet serenity fades away: He breaks into a trot, the movement of leaving all behind, of relaxation. Your horse is giggling with pleasure. He is seeking the contact, pushing himself into a slight tensile stretch. No time to look about himself now. He is invigorated. His legs rise in a diagonal solid two-beat rhythm. He bounces off the ground with power as if the earth should revolve like a ball beneath you.

Only the horseman will have knowledge of infinite weightlessness. Only he will taste the incredible joy, the first order of life, to proclaim it as in play. Only he will live for this moment, and he must indeed live for it, or it will be gone.

Nothing remains unchanged. Everything follows that which slips away, relentlessly. Everything is implacable and nevertheless harnessed by your willpower. The breath of the universe is brushing against your temples, coolly, sharply, and yet, soothingly. The world is pouring forth in your eyes. On your right and left, the countryside is spinning past you like two gigantic wheels. Everything is flowing – to that which springs eternal.

Your horse's feet are pushing off the ground and you leave behind all that is past. The earth is parting with you. The here and now directs your motion on its finest cutting edge.

You are weightless as his power is collecting under you. The play of his muscles is void of restraint. The support ahead of you is lightly held in front of the two of you. Between your horse's two-beat footfall, he lingers in weightless carriage in which none of his feet touch the ground, in which gravity is annulled.

Be like the orbit of a star to your horse's gaits. Bends and turns, tracks as straight as an arrow, beginning and end, unmeasurable poetry of movement, live power, are placed Into your feeling hands, your swinging body, and your weightless heart.

Do not interfere with the stellar orbit. Beware the moment of your tampering! – Be filled with dread of it. Behold! Behold the moment, my beloved! Behold weightlessness! Behold it like a beautiful notion that travels on the back of a star. But only the most precious blood will give you all that.

Are you returning to serenity? To maximum tranquility? Is the melody of the walk cradling you more deeply?

Vapors of sweat rise behind your horse's ears, rise from his shoulder as his nostrils blow a fine mist into the morning. The intense intriguing odeur of your horse dissipates around you and entrances you. Give him his right, entrust him with his power.

You are offering your inner self more profoundly, with greater joy, without reservation, without anything to restrain you. The right of giving yourself to the world is entering you. Pride overruns you and swells your veins. Your wrists, your ankles, your neck are cool, but your cheeks, your breasts, your thighs are heated by the pleasure of having it all.

Ride in the deepest melody of the walk, in the mist of fragrance, in the joy of having it all.

M ay the canter always be the highest moment to you. Movement of greatest beauty to the lady rider, the gait of ascent and graceful descent, majestic and smooth all in one.

In the quiet free canter, hardly moved from your seat near the withers, you only feel the balanced rhythm of the almost indistinguishable three- and four-beat footfall of your horse's pace.

Trust this movement in the right situation and in difficult situations. Your horse will carry you securely if you trust him. And if you ride across the fields, and over an obstacle, strike up a solid canter and do not attempt to carry your horse. Allow him to carry you.

But when Mohammed fled from Mecca to Medina with his couriers, their horses were on the run. All night long. Close to the ground, no longer elevating themselves, only supported in their straightforward flight by feet which touched the ground far apart, driven forward by hooves reaching far ahead of them, their bodies in a mad rush. Their tails were carried horizon-tally in the draft of their movement. Their necks stretched parallel to the horizon like steering rudders and cut through the air. Their movement was a storm, their hoofbeat was buried in its thunder. Inclined forward, as if riding weightlessly on arrows, the men sat without moving. Streams of hot air emerged from wideopen nostrils, and the desert air slashed through their exposed invulnerable lungs like a knife. Without power, stillness torn apart rushed in behind the racing horses. There, the blood of the beast was prepared to make its utmost sacrifice. They ran as if they knew that life was at stake, and it was the life of the prophet that was in danger. But they ran like confirmed race horses, they ran for man in a race between life and death.

Photo by Rik Van Lent, Jr.

Your horse is your friend. You shall not ask this utmost sacrifice in vain, or in frivolity. Leave this to the jockeys on the race track, or to prophets in flight. But you shall know of his utmost limits because women shall know of the utmost, even if it is not within their bounds.

The heavens are far above, the earth is vast. When you are three feet higher above the ground than other men, you will gain an eternal sense of this. This feeling will never leave you.

But I, my beloved, must leave you now. Your horse will be your comfort. Do not become invaded by the blabbering of obtuse riding companions. The heavens are high, the earth is grand, and they are neither as cheerful nor as earnest as your horse. Ride alone. Chat with your horse as you have learned to do. Others will bombard your mind with their words, but your horse will not offend you. And after all, my beloved, to whom else could we reveal that we are in love with each other?

Photo by Rik Van Lent, Jr.